I0409519

Your Money Your Future

A Simple Guide To Creating A Plan For Your Financial Future

By

Jameson Parker

Jameson Parker

Your Money Your Future

Introduction

Have you been thinking of a way to make a standard future for yourself? A future where you can cater for yourself, have fun with your loved ones, and enjoy a happy life.

Well, our success in life depends on our daily goals, our road map to our vision, and how we stick to the plans. Setting a financial goal is not something that can happen overnight. Everything in this life needs time, energy, perseverance, and hard work.

You can not become a rich person overnight, but there are some simple, and nice strategies you can follow to achieve your goal. Welcome to this guide to personal finance. In the following chapters, we'll look into the basic things you need to know for you to be able to take absolute possession of your financial future.

There are some basic tips you need to map out if you want to work on your finances, they include: saving, budgeting, investment, and many more. When we make saves it helps us during rainy days. How we budget for things we do spend our money plays a great role in our financial stability.

Imagine a scenario whereby we spend our money whenever we want without saving up a few amounts either in your savings box, the biggest, local banks, or many more. You need to understand the fundamental importance of saving, making budgeting you can afford, and the purpose of investing.

Your Money Your Future

Investment is a really good way of helping ourselves, especially during hard times. These are the main reasons why these three basic fundamental works hand in hand if you want to be financially stable. By the end of this book, you'll have all the knowledge and tools you need to make smart financial decisions and reach your goals.

You need to understand the fact that personal finance is a complex, and most of the time a fierce topic, but it doesn't have to be. With the right information and tools, anyone can take control of their financial future.

In this book, you will learn everything you need to in other to make an informed decision about your money. This book is designed to provide you with everything you need to make informed decisions about your money.

This book is created for anyone who dreams of taking charge of their finances and making smart decisions about their money. Whether you're just getting underway in your career or you're closing retirement, this book will give you the knowledge and mechanisms you need to catch up with your financial dreams.

Chapter One

Definition Of Personal Finance

Before we embark on any joy, first and foremost we need to know the meaning of what we are about to do. Have you asked yourself a very good question as someone who wants to set a financial goal, What personal finance is about?
We need to understand the main meaning of personal finance, then we can now know the basic steps and things we need to do. Personal finance is all about the governance of our money and assets.

It also plays a great function in things like income, spending, saving, and investing. By having proper insight, and understanding, and being able to handle these areas of personal finance, you can easily straighten up your financial situation and complete your dreams.
Let look into Income. We know that Income is the money that comes into a person's life, whether it's from our daily job, assets, or other conceptions. Having a stable income is vital for acquiring financial stability.

There are numerous different ways to increase income, including finding a higher-paying job, starting a side hustle, or investing money. Spending is another scenario we need to look into. What is spending, and want impact does it have on our finances? Spending has to do with the money that goes out of a person's life, whether it's for rent, groceries, bills, or other expenses.

Your Money Your Future

Being able to learn how to take control of our spending plays an important role in maintaining personal finances. There are some ways you can create smooth tips on the way you spend such as creating budgets, looking for a way to save up money more, and also being able to avoid impulse purchases.

Let's understand the importance of saving to our finances. Saving is the act of putting money aside for future use, whether it's for an emergency fund, a major purchase, or retirement.
It's important to have enough money saved up to cover unpredictable expenses, and it's also vital to start saving early for long-term goals.

One good method to save money is to automate the technique, by setting up direct deposits or automatic transfers from a checking account to a savings account. With these, you can be able to save more than you spend.

Investing is another key way of obtaining a standard fiance. Investing is looking for a way to grow your money over time. It can involve things like stocks, bonds, mutual funds, and other monetary tools. Investing can be risky, but it can also be an incredible way to create assets and attain your financial goals.

Chapter Two

Three Types of Financial Goals

When on the verge of starting your financial journey, there are some basic things that you need to know such as the the three main types of financial goals. Well, in the context of the investment system, financial goals are classified into long-term financial goals (goals that take up to more than 10 years to accomplish), Mid-term financial goals(goals that take up to three to ten years to accomplish), and finally the short term financial goals(goals that take not less than three years to get fulfilled).

Comprehending these three financial dreams will help you a lot when planning your investment for a brighter future. This will help you determine whether your goals a long-term, mid-term, or short-term goals.

These will play a great role in letting you be more specific with your goals. Just as setting a time structure for your investments will permit you to strategics more effectively, having clear, naturalistic time frames for the rest of your financial goals will better prepare you to program the phases you need to take to roll nearer to each one.

Long-Term Goals

As we all know long-term financial goals take more time to be fulfilled which includes ensuring financial guard in retirement or paying off your mortgage, are further a good criterion of long-term goals. Your long-term financial purposes often include several years of short-term or mid-term goals. It's always a good idea to break down large goals into smaller, more immediate goals.

Short-Term Goals

Short-term financial planning is planning that is made in less than one year or one year. You can choose to draw a plan for your business or set a goal to reach a specific amount of savings before the year's end.

You need to be able to give your financial planning or goals specific, and also a lovely name that conjures up an image, and feeling that thrills us. The great importance of financial psychology to help you reach your goals is partially in the way it encourages you to be able to see the future and feel the taste of success and how it looks. This also has to do with all of your financial goals, not just your short-term goals.

Mid-term Goals

The mid-term goals are plans set in a way that is greater than one year but won't take up to five to one years before being accomplished. This type of plan is being made to provide medium-term funds that are required for the maintenance of assets, acquisition of additional equipment, and the running of R&O activities, as well as providing your additional working capital.

You may want to explore ways to generate passive income or hire a financial advisor to help you plan your retirement. Each of these examples of mid-term financial goals has a time frame of three to ten years and is ultimately a stepping stone to a larger goal.

Chapter Three

Vision

Before you can be able to set up your financial goal, the first thing you have to do is to set up your vision for the future. Making and creating your vision plays a crucial role in determining how you want your future to look. Vision has to do with how you want your life will be like in the next 5 to 10 years.

Well, our vision can something change due to one reason or the other, but in this aspect, you can also try to amend your plans. Our vision varies based on the way we lay our path. You need to spend some time to understand what you want, this will create a path for you to know what you are working on.

One of the ways you can create a good vision for yourself is by asking yourself vital questions. Questions like in my 80 years, how do I tell people the best part of my life during my youthful time, and many more.

What type of memory would like to create for yourself that will make people around you wish to behave or draw inspiration from you? Well, doing this will help you in setting very good goals for yourself, and also be a point of motivation as you work towards your plans.

Your Money Your Future

In a case whereby we don't know what we want in our life for the betterment of our future can sweep us away with someone else vision. For instance, many people are selling numerous products and other valuable stuff. These people tend to know what works best for them, and they can as well be able to figure out their vision.

Trying to do things in a way that works for other people might sometimes favor you, but in most cases won't end up very well. Working on someone else vision is something you need to avoid in some aspect especially when your not making it just like them.

The best thing you need to do for yourself is to sit down, relax, and think about things that will suit you as a person. Knowing our weaknesses, abilities, and many qualities about our personal life is a good way we can be able to know how can be able to work towards our path. Once you can be able to understand your vision, the next step you need to take is to hold to it.

For instance, your vision might be to own a house before your 30s. All you have to do is work very hard in a way that will help you achieve your dream and become that person you have been dreaming of.

Chapter Four

Road Map

Setting up your vision is not just enough, you need to also create what we call a road map. A road map is a strategy that will help you in achieving your personal goals, and the right path to follow in other to reach success.

Without bringing up a strategy that will help us reach our destination, we might end up standing still or losing focus along the way. Success is not something that can occur as magic without some good qualities like hard work, perseverance, time, and the act of seriousness.

Understanding these qualities will help you a lot in attaining your personal financial goals. In this aspect, you need to ask yourself some questions like do I need to save up a lot at some point then quit, and then do some work abroad? Or do I need to make more money and build up my passive income online while providing value at the same time? Well, it all knowing how your strategy ought to be and how you can work towards that plan.

Your Money Your Future

Chapter Five

Setting Up Or Writing Down Your Goals

Writing down your goals is a good way of laying your foundation on how to build your personal finance goals. Writing your goals down makes it significant, and more likely that you will be able to achieve them.

It is easier to remember what we have penned or written down than something we have of mind or head. There are several ways or places you can write down your goals which can be digital or manually.

You can also do a combination of both. You can have some written on your notepad, book, journal, spreadsheet, and many more.

Setting up a goal is a vital thing you need to seriously work on if you intend to reach a good mile while working towards your financial goals. There are three main goals setting tips you need to know, which includes:

How Many Goals To Set, And How to Set Them

Well, it's undeniable that we have numerous goals that we want to work on, but the main thing we need to do is to learn how to recognize them. Different things will come up in different ways demanding more or less time in some ways. Whether it is a day job, kids, and many more.

According to research, the perfect number of goals you need to set for yourself in a year is three. You need to focus all your energy, time, and hard work on them. Well, you can choose your three, and try to break them down into a time phrase.

For instance one of your main goals is to save up to $12,000 or $20,000 this year. Instead of you not fulfilling your goal because of some certain problem you might face along the way. You can choose to break it down by choosing to save $3,000 in three months, the same goes for the next three months, and so on.

You can change this strategy depending on how you choose to break things down for yourself in a way that will suit you.

Lead Measures

The lead measure is one of the key formulas you need to abide by while making or setting your financial goals. Well, in this place, this is where most people get things wrong. One of the biggest mistakes that people normally make while setting their goals is focusing only on the outcome, forgetting the process.

For instance, while playing basketball, and you focus only on the scoreboard you will entirely lose focus and interest. But if you focus on the tips, and strategy that will help you gain more points to win the game will sky rock your motive enabling you to aim more for the win.

The same thing goes for us while making plans and setting our personal finance goals. If you intend to save up to $10,000 in three months and you keep on staring at your bank account without working or adding more cash to your bank account, you will end up without any proper outcome.

No magic will increase your balance if you don't think of a way to save up. All you have to do is to put more focus on your lead measure. Your lead measure can be working extra hours, cutting down your expenses, and how you spend money. By doing this the goal will naturally take care of itself, then checking your bank balance all the time, hoping for a miracle to occur.

Accountable Partner

Having an accountable partner is another surefire way of reaching your dream destination for your financial goals. Having someone by your side such as your best friend, parent, sibling, husband, wife, or anyone you wish to will help you a lot in reaching your goals.

Having an accountable partner will help you check how you are moving with your plans, and also help you by encouraging you to reach your financial goal.

Imagine a scenario whereby Team A has no goals or plans, while Team B has a written goal, and no plan Team C has written goals and a clear plan, and Team D has written goals, clear plans, and an accountable partner.

Among these four teams which team do you think will reach and meet their personal finance goals? We all know that it's team D, the team with written goals, clear plans, and an accountable partner.

That's to show you the great value of having someone by your side, who you will be giving account for on your personal goals which you can check in every day, week, and month

Your Money Your Future

Chapter Six

How to Set Financial Goals

Do you ever feel that you are working tirelessly to spend wisely with your financial resources but you are never successful? Or have you been putting your tail off, but at the end of the month, you don't have anything to show for it?

Yes, issues like inflation and recession are genuine concerns that might seem like major impediments. But even when the economy isn't insane, if you don't establish any financial objectives, you'll probably still feel like you're going nowhere.

You need to establish some financial dreams if you want to commence moving forward with your money. It's not as difficult as it sounds, so don't worry. Let me take you step-by-step through the methodology of setting financial dreams.

What Do You Comprehend By The Word Financial Goal?

Any procedure you bear for handling your money is a financial goal. Long-term financial pursuit, such as investing for retirement, can be either short-term (such as saving up $1,000) or long-term. Every room of your life should have purposes, but owning straightforward financial pursuits can support you put your money where your prerogatives are.

Also, I cannot discuss financial pursuits without saying the Baby Steps. Making financial determinations may be as problematic as determining what to watch on Netflix. There are so numerous picks, and everyone has a preference.

Do you need to pay off debt? Do you put money aside for your children's college? buying a home? Investing for the future? Your road to completing all of those tasks is made apparent by the 7 Baby Steps, which cut through the muddle. In order to achieve more progress with your money and enjoy financial calm, it helps you concentrate on one objective at a time.

In order to find out what Baby Step you're on, take this fast survey if you have no idea what financial objective to pursue first.

Ways to Set Financial Goals in 5 Easy Steps

1. Specify your objective.

Too vague aims are one of the reasons individuals fail to accomplish their objectives. I wish to handle money better, you may say. What does it, nevertheless, mean to you? Reduce the scope!

What if you choose to pay off your debt instead? To concentrate on that particular area of your finances. Let's now discuss how to further deconstruct this aim.

2. Make your objective quantifiable.

So you want to pay off your debt, okay? Now is the moment to choose a precise amount—something you can quantify to find out whether or not you achieved your objective.

Your ultimate objective should be to be debt-free in full (this is Baby Step 2), but it's a good idea to split that goal down into smaller pieces. You won't feel too defeated before you even begin in this manner.

Therefore, even though you may have a total debt of $30,000, you would like to start by paying off a $15,000 student loan. Hey, that's an attainable objective!

3. Establish a due date.

Let's get to it: If your goals don't have a deadline, it's quite tempting to put them off. There are seven days in a week, and someday is not one of them. Don't keep saying someday. You must set a deadline for yourself that is both acceptable and moderately difficult.

Resuming the student loan illustration When do you hope to reach your objective? You'll need to pay $1,250 every month if you want to pay off $15,000 in a year. Is this conceivable but also a little bit unrealistic? Good if so!

4.Make sure they are your own objectives.

Let's have a little discussion regarding comparison. It's simple to observe what other people are doing and assume that you ought to follow suit. Do your neighbors have the newest models of vehicles? Does that one gal who posts on Instagram usually go on fancy vacations? Hey, congrats to them! However, it does not follow that you must follow suit.

We are playing a game we can never win when we evaluate ourselves in relation to other people. Therefore, be sure the financial objectives you establish are appropriate for you. In other words, you shouldn't take out a second mortgage simply because all of your friends are doing it for newly remodeled kitchens. Put on your blinders, pay attention to your lane, and sprint to the finish line. And be specific about the reasons behind your objective selection.

5. Outline your objective.

Did you know that writing down your goals will increase your chances of success? It's true what they say about writing things down helping you focus on what's important at hand.

Put your objectives down on paper now. After that, attach them to your desk, bathroom mirror, or automobile. To make sure you see them right away when you pick up your phone, type them into the Notes app on your phone, take a screenshot, and set it as your wallpaper. You'll remain inspired and on target if you maintain your goals in plain sight.

Chapter Seven

5 Characteristic Financial Goals

With so extensively funds "suggestion" swimming around, it can be hard to know which financial pursuits are good for you. To specify your long-term financial aim, start with the baby steps, as I previously advised. More diminutive goals, though, might also nurse you in achieving those milestones.

The most typical financial objectives people have are listed here, along with advice on how to win them.

1. Establish and follow a budget.

Budgeting is one of the top financial resolutions individuals make each year, and it's also the base around that you should construct all other financial objectives.

Having a financial plan is necessary for financial success. It is a strategy to control your sources of income and expenditures. You are managing your money rather than wondering where it is.

For you to be aware of the fact that you are getting closer to your goal every month. By making a budget, you may improve all aspects of your financial situation. If you already follow a budget, congrats! If not, sign up right now for Every Dollar without cost.

2. Create a cash reserve.

Your Money Your Future

In life, unexpected things happen. However, if you have enough money saved up, you may be prepared for any monetary problems that might happen. I'm referring to the hardest parts of growing up, like driving.

As a starting point for your finances, decide to save $1,000. Now is the time to pay off whatever debts you may have at that time. (I'll explain it in greater depth.)

The next step is to create an emergency fund that is completely funded and has enough money to cover costs for three to six months. (Again, the Baby Steps, the tried-and-true way to help you retrieve governance of your finances, cover all of this.)

Having a crisis fund is necessary to be ready for such "life happens" scenarios. You won't be concerned about what could occur in the future since you will be confident that you have the cash on hand stored up to handle it.

3. Pay off your debts.

If you have debt, now is the moment to take it seriously and pay it off. Absolutely everything. Yes, I am aware it may currently appear difficult, particularly in light of the large figures that are in front of you.

On the other hand, debt holds you back rather than advancing you. If all of your income is going into bills, you cannot go ahead financially.
If you want to make more money available for your goals. You will learn precisely how to complete the Baby Steps and get out of debt for good in this course.

4. Put money aside for your ideal retirement.

Visualize your fantasy retirement for a beat. Would you like to take the grandchildren to Disney World each Christmas? Once every three months, take your partner to a different state. Finished all the books on your shelves? Start an enjoyable hobby.

Whatever your prospective plans are, you'll need wise retirement investing today to make them a reality. Therefore, I like you to commence today saving 15% of your family payment for retirement as shortly as you are without any debt and have that emergency fund completely built. And what's this? All the funds you were clearing off debt is now the power for your retirement dreams when you are debt-free.

5.Save more, and spend less

Many individuals say things like, "I want to spend less" or "I want to save more" without really considering what such statements entail. However, you need to be conscious of your spending patterns.

Develop a spending plan for each month that you adhere to, shop for discounts, use coupons, and pay with cash. Here's a significant one: Learn to refuse yourself, too! I'm not saying you shouldn't enjoy yourself. Nevertheless, money savings will need some preparation and lifestyle changes.

Finally, here's one of my most popular recommendations for cutting expenses and increasing savings: Construct a food plan! Meal planning may help you reduce your spending on food, which is where most people go beyond.

Your Money Your Future

Chapter Eight

An Example of a Financial Goal in

Action

Okay, now that I've covered the fundamentals of financial goal planning, allow me to give you an illustration of how this may function in practice. My partner Frank and I decided the decision to construct a home a while back.

Before then, whatever additional funds we received were immediately deposited into our general savings. But I was aware that building a house would be expensive, and unforeseen costs would inevitably arise. We therefore set ourselves the objective of saving as much money as we could, primarily for our home.

Even though saving up so much money seemed nearly impossible, setting monthly objectives for it helped us gain so much momentum. Our desire was made achievable by having a strategy for our finances, which also made the process enjoyable.

It also helped me to control my spending habits (also known as dependencies; believe me, they exist). I was inspired to cut back on my spending since I knew my money was going toward something I desired. Finding innovative methods to reach our goal more quickly kept us on track each month, even if there were times when we felt worn out—I mean, there were days when all I wanted to do was rest and spend money.

Beyond that, it developed character. We can always look back on that period of our marriage and be proud of what we managed to do as a team. It facilitated a link between us and satisfaction in our lives.

Chapter Nine

Why are financial goals important?

Investing targets are essential for several encouragements:

Financial targets furnish your investment efforts guidance and meaning. Because you are aware of the dream you are aiming towards, they make it simpler for you to make sacrifices or keep to a spending plan. They assist you in maintaining long-term attention.

Financial pursuits provide you with direction and drive, and they may also keep you focused on your money-management strategy. The pursuit you set should be significant to you so that they may motivate you to continue pursuing them.

Accountability - Putting all of your targets in writing and holding yourself responsible for your accomplishments (whether simply to you or a significant other) keeps you honest about how you are doing. You can stay on track by evaluating your dreams frequently.

Achievement - You feel successful when you achieve your financial ideals. Celebrating important anniversaries is also beneficial.

Your Money Your Future

Finding innovative methods to reach our purpose more quickly kept us on track each month despite our exhaustion—I mean, there were days when all I wanted to do was rest and spend cash.

A plan gives you something to work for and makes you more financially savvy. As time goes on, you'll begin to see how each choice you make affects your total financial situation.

For instance, it's not a huge concern to buy breakfast and coffee every day if you don't have any financial ambitions. Let's examine the exact cost to you of it, though. You'll normally spend at least $15 on lattes for just one workweek, which works up to $50 every month! What other uses could you have for that cash?

Compound interest may cause your $100 monthly investment to increase to more than $7,000 if you invest that money for five years. You are drinking during your children's whole college term.

Think about investing $100 every month for 15 years if you had an even longer time horizon. You may end up with nearly $45,000 in savings from lattes. How would your investments fare if you waited 30 years to invest? Your coffee budget can increase to more than $280,000. Would you rather have a daily latte or $250,000? I don't drink coffee all that often, but I do like a nice cup.

Find modest (or significant) sacrifices you can make right away to position yourself for financial security. Your future will be impacted by what you do with your money now in day-to-day life.

With targets you can fulfill what you want to accomplish Building goals for money will assist you in changing your perspective your routines and eventually your life. You can stretch your budget further by being deliberate with every dollar you have.

As a result, you may accomplish more of what you want to do and make plans for what you do in the future. You're capable of doing more than you ever imagined but developing financial pursuits can help you get there, and determine the future you wish to have and the steps you must take now to achieve it.

Instead of the bank rules, you may live your life. Debt is something that you can permanently eliminate. The ability to accumulate wealth will allow you to finance important purchases the way you set your financial objectives depends on a variety of factors including your upbringing your driving forces and your future aspirations bear in mind, it all begins with a budget.

This is the basis. It's the strategy. And it's how you get deliberate with your money. Go ahead and start your free budget today with Every-dollar. Then, start taking the necessary actions to fulfill your financial goals. You may make these aspirations come true at any time of year. Get it now!

Your Money Your Future

Chapter Ten

Conclusion

There is a good chance that none of your goals will be attained in a perfectly linear fashion but the main thing is to stay consistent. Don't be upset with yourself if you have to withdraw money out of your emergency fund one month because you have an unanticipated auto repair or medical cost.

That's why the fund is there just as soon as you can begin going again a similar situation arises. If you are ill or lose your work to get through that challenging time you'll need to come up with a new plan you might not be able to pay off debt or put money away for retirement. During that time you can restart your original plan or possibly a revised one when things go back to normal.

The guidance of financial planning is the point that you can update your goals as you take control of your progress despite all the ups and downs in life. However, in this aspect, you can be able to discover those things either small or big things you can do on a day-to-day, monthly, or annually basis to guarantee that your financial future is safe.

www.ingramcontent.com/pod-product-compliance
Lightning Source LLC
Chambersburg PA
CBHW072227290526
45794CB00007B/2920